GW00646687

DEAR
MUM

M·I·L·K

Edited by
Geoff Blackwell

Abrams, London
in association with PQ Blackwell

All that
I am
or ever hope to be,
I owe to
my angel
mother.

Abraham Lincoln

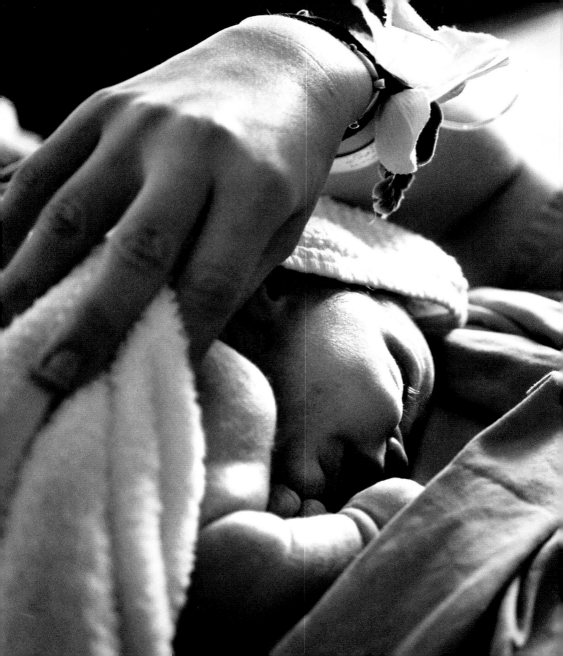

Life began

by waking up and

loving my

mother's face.

George Eliot

My mother

is a never-ending song in my heart of comfort, happiness and being. I may sometimes forget the words but I *always* remember the tune.

Graycie Harmon

Mothers
are all slightly
insane.

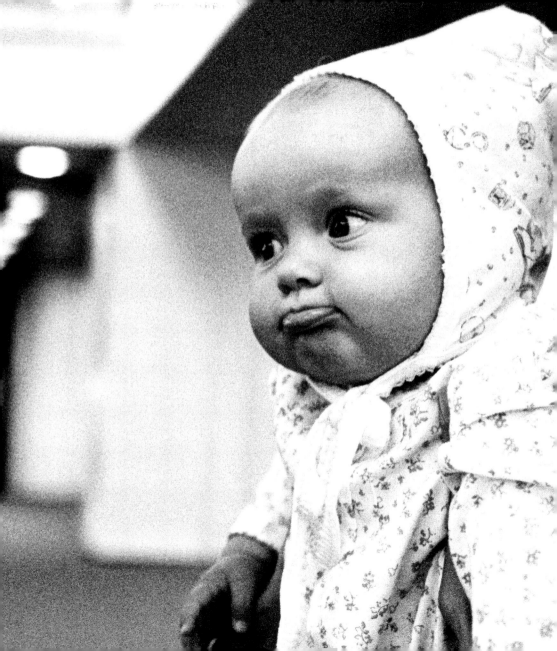

To a child's ear,
'mother' is
magic
in any language.

Arlene F Benedict

A mother is a person
who seeing there are only
four pieces of pie
for five people,
promptly announces she never did care for pie.

Tenneva Jordan

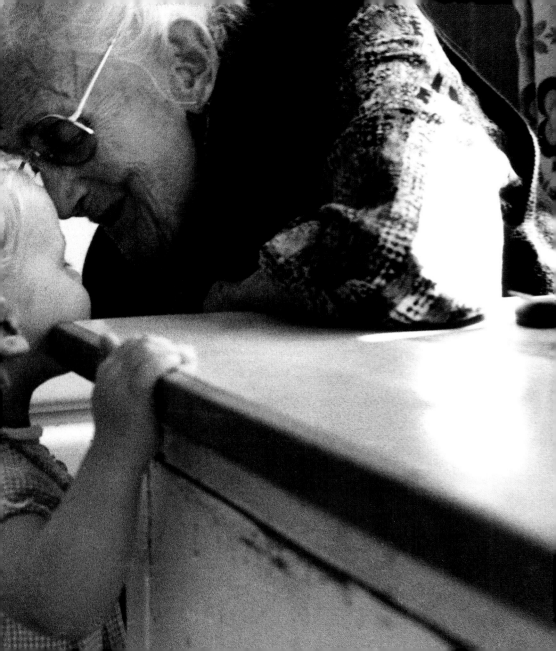

A mother is

not to be compared with any other person – she is

incomparable.

If I know
what love is,
it is because of
you.

Hermann Hesse

A mother holds

her children's hands for a while...

their *hearts* forever.

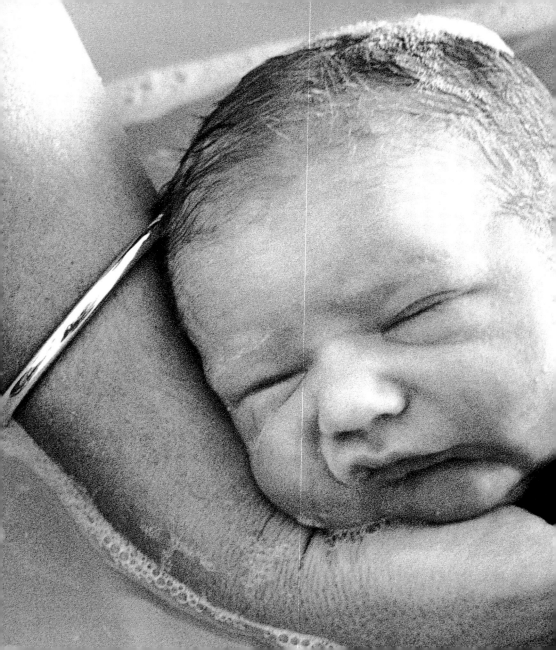

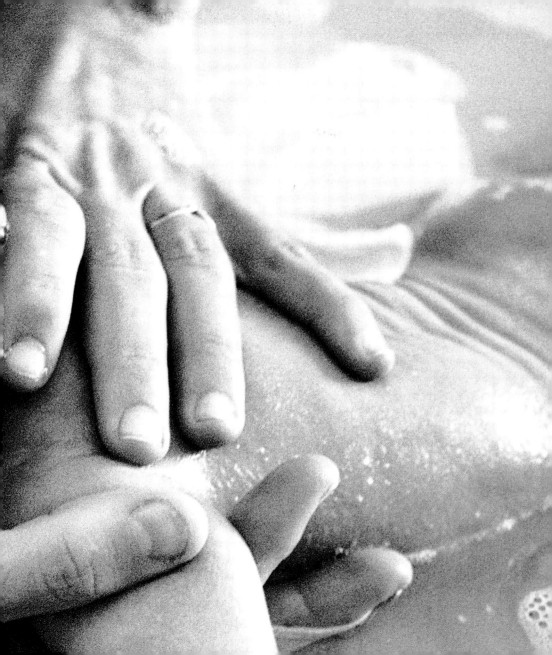

A mother's
love
liberates.

If at first
you don't
succeed,
do it
the way your
mother
told you to.

It was when I had *my* first child
that I understood
how much
my mother
loved me.

My mother is as beautiful as a princess, as fierce as a lioness. My mother is magic.

Ella Jacobson

My mother
had a slender, small body,
but a large heart —
a heart so large that
everybody's joys
found welcome in it and
hospitable accommodation.

Mark Twain

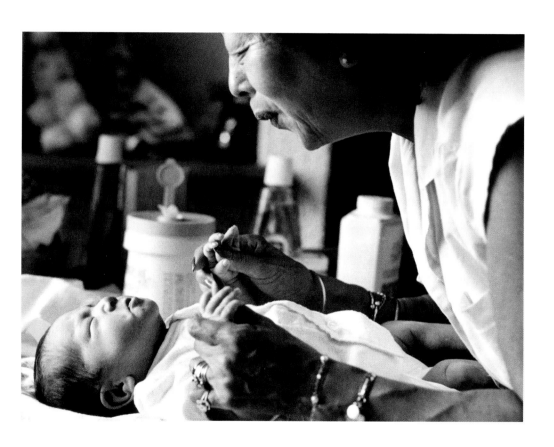

The patience
of a mother
might be likened
to a tube of toothpaste –
it's never
quite all gone.

Mothers are *fairy tales* of happily ever after.

© Paolo Sapio, Italy
A self-portrait of the photographer's hands.

© David White, UK
Photographed in Bristol, UK, the photographer's wife sees their two-minute-old son, Louie, for the first time.

© Nico Sepe, Sri Lanka
The photographer's four-month-old daughter, Olivia, is cuddled by her mother, Maeve.

© Meg Venter, USA
The photographer and her baby daughter, Wren, play in their living room.

© Fabien Raes, Belgium
Sonja has just given birth in the water to her fourth child Manon at the Henri Serruys Clinic in Oostende, Belgium.

© Guan Cheong Wong, Malaysia
Front and back – in the Cameron Highlands, Malaysia, a mother carries her children in the traditional way of the Orang Asli people.

© Kamthorn Pongsutiyakorn, Thailand
A grandmother with her grand-daughter in the backyard of their home in Chonburi, Thailand.

© Roberto Colacioppo, Italy
A great-grandmother's heartfelt embrace of a young bride. The old lady, ninety-seven, and her great-granddaughter are the only family members who still live in the mountain village of Roccaspinalveti, Italy.

© Manfred Wirtz, Netherlands
In a remote area of Romania, a new bride is dressed by her mother and three sisters. The ceremony symbolizes that she is leaving home to start a new life with her husband.

© Álvaro Diaz, Brazil
Ten-month-old Gabriel and his mother, Paula. The photographer captured this picture of his son in Florianopolis, Brazil.

© Stefano Azario, UK
Like mother, like daughter – at a New York airport, there's still time for nine-month-old Verity and her mother, Lydzia, to play before the long flight home to the UK.

© Len Speier, USA
The photographer's wife, Joan, and their son, Jonathan, at home in New York, USA.

© Stacy Wasmuth, USA
Wearing remarkably similar expressions, Evelyn and her great-grandson, Micah, meet for the first and last time at Evelyn's nursing home in Chillicothe, Ohio, USA.

© Andrew Lichtenstein, USA
Three generations – mother, Linda, daughter, Jade, and grandmother, Sharon – share an affectionate moment on a late-summer afternoon in New Hampshire's White Mountains, Western Maine, USA.

© Venkata Sunder Rao Pampana (Sunder), India
A tender touch – a young girl looks after her baby sister asleep in a hammock made from her mother's sari. Without a permanent home, the family lives on the streets of Vijayawada in India.

© Nancy Clendaniel, USA
After missing a catch during a baseball game in Renton, Washington, USA, a little boy runs to his mother for comfort.

© Stephanus Meyer, Spain
A young single mother takes a break to feed her baby. She is a farm worker in the Karoo region, South Africa.

© Auke Vleer, Netherlands
Young cousins – Pol, Joris, Dorus and Rik – enjoy being taken for a ride on the beach in Baratier, France.

© Anne Anderson, USA
One-year-old Grace shows off her crawling prowess to her mother, Jamie, in their home in Indianapolis, Indiana, USA.

© Jonathan Jones, UK
The photographer's son, Oliver, and his grandma express their affection for each other.

© Katharina Brinckmeier, Netherlands
The special relationship between two-year-old Mayra and her grandmother Mutti, ninety-two, captured on film in the village of Rautheim in Braunschweig, Germany.

© Gerald Botha, South Africa
Good morning in Durban, South Africa – the photographer's wife, Aileen, greets their three-month-old son, Eden.

© Frank White, USA
In Houston, Texas, USA, Jo-Anne cuddles her five-year-old daughter, Ellen, in a loving and protective embrace. They are smiling at the photographer – husband and father Frank White.

© Anne Bayin, Canada
Kim Phuc was the subject of the most famous picture of the Vietnam War. Taken in 1972, that photograph showed Kim – 'the girl in the picture' – badly burned by napalm. Kim grew up thinking boys would find her unattractive because of her scars, but today she is married and living in Canada. She is a Goodwill Ambassador for UNESCO. This photograph celebrates the first birthday of Kim's son, Thomas.

© Jarek Kret, Poland
In a remote village on the west coast of Madagascar, a young woman is oblivious to the photographer's presence as he captures this tender image of her watching over her young child.

© Linda Heim, USA
Lynn and her ten-month-old son, Casey, try a new variation of rock-a-bye-baby on the shore of Burden Lake in New York state, USA.

© Sayyed Nayyer Reza, Pakistan
Love and kindness bridge the generation gap in Lahore, Pakistan. Nine-year-old Suman shares a playful moment with her elderly friend and neighbour – the old lady is known simply as Amman, an Urdu word for 'mother'.

© Milo Stewart Jr, USA
In Cooperstown, New York, new mother Leslie is enchanted with her baby son, Bartow.

© Mark LaRocca, USA
A mother's joyous smile as she admires her newborn baby, Cedric, born thirty-six hours ago at this hospital in Newton, Massachusetts, USA.

© Krisadakorn Chaiyaphaka, Thailand
A portrait of love and contentment in Chiang Rai, Thailand, as a young woman bathes and feeds her baby son.

© Melissa Mermin, USA
On her wedding day, the bride, Jessica, hugs her mother whose own wedding portrait hangs above the mantelpiece in her home in North Stonington, Connecticut, USA.

© Fiona Morrison, Australia
The photographer's two-year-old daughter, Mahli, makes friends with Holly, a visitor newly arrived in Darwin, Australia.

© Kelvin Patrick Jubb, Australia
Fewer than twenty-four hours have elapsed since this baby was born. In a busy hospital ward in Penrith, Australia, the baby is cradled by his mother as he experiences his first bath.

© Lynn Goldsmith, USA
A little girl holds tightly to her grandmother's hand as they walk together in Arles, France.

© Russell Shakespeare, Australia
In Manly, New South Wales, Australia, five-month-old Camille has a captive audience in her mother, Toni, and visiting grandparents, Margaret and Handley.

© Fredé Spencer, Denmark
Water baby – swimming under water comes perfectly naturally to baby Louis. He and his mother, Dimiti, enjoy a swimming class for 'Little Dippers' in London, UK.

© Thomas Patrick Kiernan, Ireland
A young boy shares his delight with his mother as he paddles in the water on Coney Island, New York, USA.

© Wilfred van Zyl, South Africa
Six-year-old Marcelle holds on tight as her father, the photographer, takes her for a spin. To achieve the effect, Wilfred van Zyl strapped the camera to his chest and used the self-timer to capture his daughter's delighted smile as he swings her through the air. The reflection of the photographer can be seen in the little girl's eyes.

© Sam Lim, Malaysia
The photographer's son, Lim-Kenji, clips his grandmother's fingernails.

© Shauna Angel Blue, USA
Chicago, Illinois, USA – dressed in her favourite tutu, two-year-old Rose dances to the tune of her mother's harp.

© Eddee Daniel, USA
A moment of discovery in Sauk City, Wisconsin, USA, as one-year-old Chelsea realizes where the music is coming from.

© Juan P Barragán, Ecuador
Keeping tradition alive near Lake San Pablo, Ecuador. Four generations of an Imbabura Indian family prepare their hair in the time-honoured way – from right to left: Mama-Rosa, Rosa, Rosa Elena and Miriam.

© Lloyd Erlick, Canada
Family portrait in Toronto, Canada – proud mother Caitlin gently holds six-month-old Shai as she reaches out to greet her great-grandmother, Natalie.

© Linda Sole, UK
When her daughter, Judith, became pregnant, Linda Sole decided to make this her next project. Judith is enjoying a bath on a hot summer day in Woolwich, London, UK – two months later a daughter, Rose, was born.

© Ário Gonçalves, Brazil
In Alvorado, Brazil, a gentle kiss from her mother, Rosângela, elicits a happy gurgle from three-month-old Ariane.

© Jodi Durow, USA
The photographer's friend, Caroline, has finally managed to get her three-week-old daughter, Catherine, off to sleep.

© Pietro Sutera, Germany
A bucket of cold water makes a welcome shower on a hot day for a little girl in Cape Town, South Africa.

© Guus Rijven, Netherlands
Holiday in the countryside of La Romagne, France – freezing temperatures, hungry woodstoves and just enough hot water for the kitchen sink. Four-month-old Jarón is quite happy to be washed alongside the pots and pans.

© Gautam Basu, India
In the village of Narsingpur in West Bengal, India, Sarojini, who comes from a family of potters, tells her grandchildren stories of her childhood.

© Yew Fatt Siew, Malaysia
A Buddhist festival at Labuleng Lamasery in Gansu, China – in sub-zero temperatures, a Tibetan mother's embrace offers protection and warmth.

© Cheryl Shoji, Canada
In Burnaby, British Columbia, Canada, proud grandmother Dorothy soothes her first grandson as he expresses displeasure at a not-so-dry diaper.

© Stacey P Morgan, USA
In New York, Anne and her young son, Robert, discover that the bedroom is the perfect place for hide and seek.

© Herman Krieger, USA
Surrounded by pictures of her loved ones, ninety-two-year-old Frances reminisces on family life at her home in Oregon, USA.

© Neil Selkirk, USA
Open wide – on a trip to the beach in Wellfleet, Massachusetts, USA, nothing interests Zane more than her mother, Susan.

© Devang Prajapati, India
In the town of Ahmedabad, India, one-year-old Forum is fascinated by the face of elderly neighbour Mrs Champaben.

© Auke Vleer, Netherlands
Five-year-old Pol with his aunt, Letty, on a family vacation in Baratier, France. While grandmother Fanny admires the view of the lake, their dog prefers to take a nap.

© Binode Kumar Das, India
After a hard day's work in West Bengal, India, a mother is delighted to return to the company of her children.

© Isabelle Heyvaert, Belgium
Veronique and Kelly share a mother-daughter moment on the beach in Het Zoute, Belgium.

© Natassa Tselepoglou, Greece
Family life in Halkidiki, Greece. Three-year-old Lia and her mother, Daphne, put their feet up and share a fairy tale.

ISBN: 978-0-810-99598-7

Produced and originated by PQ Blackwell Limited, 116 Symonds Street, Auckland, New Zealand
www.pqblackwell.com

Edited by Geoff Blackwell
Book design by Cameron Gibb

This edition first published in 2009 by Abrams UK, a subsidiary of La Martinière Groupe.

Printed by Midas Printing International, China.

10 9 8 7 6 5 4 3 2 1

Abrams books are available at special discounts when purchased in quantity for premiums and promotions as
well as fundraising or educational use. Special editions can also be created to specification. For details, contact
Abrams UK at the address below.

▲ Abrams

The Market Building
72-82 Rosebery Avenue
London EC1R 4RW
www.abramsbooks.co.uk

www.milkphotos.com